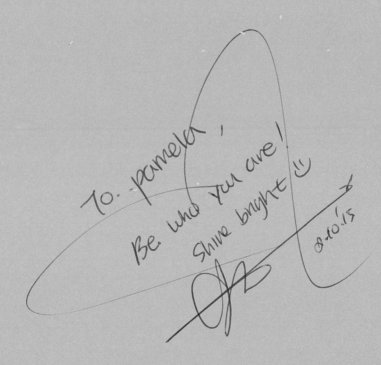

To. -pamela ,
Be who you are !
Shine bright :)

0.10.15

The Cupcake Theory

The secret ingredient to being happy
in your relationships

CLARA LEE

Foreword by Robert J. Thomas, Ph.D.

CLÚ Press; Los Angeles

ISBN 978-0-9888648-0-1

www.cupcaketheorybook.com

Library of Congress Control Number: 2013900990

First Printing, 2013

Printed on acid free eco-friendly paper with non-toxic soy inks

Printed in China

Cover and Interior Design by Deasy Suryani

For my wise parents and my awesome brother,
who taught their daughter and little sister how to
love while being a genuine individual.

사랑해요.

'I love you'

(in Korean)

Join
The Cupcake
Theory
movement.

You are invited.

CONTENTS

FOREWORD

Cupcake Theory?? My initial reaction, too. Yet it didn't take long for me to realize that Clara Lee was on to something. Like it or not, we're all attracted by the frosting. You know: the promise of something outrageously sweet and incredibly smooth. But how many times have you tasted a cupcake only to discover that the real delight was not in the frosting but in the cake? More than once, I'd bet. Clara's point exactly. How many times has the frosting disappointed you? How many times have you neglected the cake?

While this is not a book about cupcakes ... Clara did consult some of the world's foremost bakers and designers of cupcakes as she developed her theory. Why? Because bakers know something many of us forget: a great cupcake has a great foundation. Like Clara says, you need substance to support the frosting.

The same can be said for the best singers, dancers, figure-skaters, musicians, inspiring men and women everywhere. They all have substance and their substance – the things they value, the relationships they create, the love they share – is what makes them beautiful, a joy to watch and to get to know.

So, read this book. Savor the images. Reflect on the words. And as you do those things, know that the simplest pieces of advice are often the most profound. Don't be surprised if something you might have thought of as frivolous turns out to hold the key to discovering your own inner beauty.

Robert J. Thomas, Ph.D.

Writer, Teacher, Consultant of leadership and transformational change

Best Selling Author of Geeks and Geezers and Crucibles of Leadership

Writer for Harvard Business School Review and MIT Sloan Management Review

The Cupcake
Theory

the secret ingredient to being happy
in your relationships

INTRODUCTION

As individuals journeying through our lives, we seek and value self-identity and uniqueness. We want to know ourselves to be able to stand out from the rest of the human population. This process seems simple and clear; and it is, until we start letting other people into our lives to fulfill our natural human desires for romance, partnership, and love.

Why is love, a key aspect of life, so hard for many of us to maintain? Why are there so many challenges to finding love, building love, and sustaining love over time? Why is it that even when we are in a relationship, we may find ourselves unhappy as it gets more serious? Why, instead of finding a new and vibrant sense of ourselves in some relationships, do we feel more and more lost? What are the thoughts, feelings, and attitudes go into staying happy in a relationship? Is there a single, most effective solution to being happy in a relationship?

These questions can be endless. While we may find the answers to these wonders at some point in our lives, it seems that most of us never do and are left constantly falling victim to dead ends in relationships.

The key ingredient to ultimately finding happiness in our relationship, and to not end up in the shadows, with disappointment or heartbreak, is making sure to never lose ourselves. The key is to be our own solid foundation and to view our partner, not as a part of that foundation, but as a complement to it that makes the whole of us that much more desirable and exciting.

It is as simple as when you first let yourself fall for your special someone. When you decided to or fell into liking or loving your special someone, you had all the control in the world to decide to grow feelings for that person and give love a chance. You listened and paid attention to yourself and your feelings enough to know what you wanted to be with that person and acted according to what you wanted to do.

Think about this:

 You are the one who let yourself fall in love with someone.

 You are the one who let yourself open up to someone else.

 You put yourself out there.

 You chose to get in to this….

So it is your responsibility to take care of yourself, as you started all this...

It's been you - always you. Therefore you have to keep it at "you", even when you are in the relationship with someone else. You have to prioritize and take care of yourself because you are the only one who can determine your happiness and wellbeing.

That saying, "You can't love others unless you learn to love yourself" is true.

You can't just let yourself fall in love and then lose yourself by letting the other person overshadow you and your light...Your partner fell in love with you for a reason, and it's because of the person you are, so what would the point be if that person was lost along the way? The whole point of your relationship is to find your partner, your complement that can make you shine brighter and make you feel happier – they should only be your enhancer. And to maintain yourself as your own person so that your partner can continue to love you as the whole, original, and fundamental you.

This is the essence of The Cupcake Theory.

Your relationship with yourself determines your happiness and your relationship with others. Therefore we must always work to improve our relationship with ourselves in order to optimize our interpersonal relationships.

This is the key point we must remind ourselves in order to be successful in our relationships.

Now, with that being said, how do we reach this point? What if I understand this concept, yet find it hard to apply, or find myself caught up in losing myself in my partner's image of me?

Many times we may find ourselves in a situation that we know we need to get out of, yet just can't help ourselves but be stuck in it. That is because there are so many variables that make it hard to maneuver ourselves in a relationship. Even when we think we have what it takes to be centered and solid at one moment, another moment we may find ourselves cast to the other end of the spectrum. You may start to wonder if there is any way to really maintain your happiness and self-control in a relationship.

Well, there is!

There is one fun and simple rule that will cover all your bases when it comes to staying happy and simultaneously true to yourself in your relationships, and that one rule is The Cupcake Theory!

At the heart of The Cupcake Theory is the idea that each of us are our own beautiful and unique cupcake; our partner is the frosting, which further beautifies and enhances us. This unique perspective for examining our romantic relationships and ourselves, can help us gain what our hearts truly want – the amazing experiences of life and love.

While we desire to fall in love and commit to relationships, the process can be both beautiful and dangerously unpredictable. It is easy to fall into the trap of becoming dependent on our partners, eventually losing ourselves, our composure and our demanding beauty. The moment we lose sight of ourselves in a relationship, we automatically lose control of ourselves as well.

When we are in a relationship, we should be the decadent, solid, and sweet foundation, just like a perfectly baked cupcake. Our partner should be the excitement, the complementary element that adds to and evokes the best in us, just like the sprinkles and frosting on a cupcake.

This is The Cupcake Theory, and you can live it.

Because after all, whatever we do, wherever we go, and whoever we meet, we all deserve to be happy, whole, and just down right fabulous!

Consider
this Cupcake

Is There A Best Cupcake?

No! There is an infinite variety of wonderful cupcakes in the world.

 Every baker has her/his own cupcake style with a unique look and texture.

 Some love the classiness of velvet, while others love the playfulness of chocolate chip. Some relish vivid colors, while others go with a subtle and subdued approach. Some prefer rich and deep complexity, while others prefer a light and spongy delicacy.

Regardless of individual style, one thing on which they all agree is that

A cupcake as a whole has to have…

Real Substance!

THEORY OF CUPCAKES

What makes for a great cupcake?

 First, there is the cake. The cake is always the first priority.

 Then there is the frosting. Frosting is great, but it always comes second. The focus is first and foremost the cake.

What does "real substance" mean?
Well, a cupcake should

 Be able to hold its own,

 Have a solid foundation.

 Have a look of its own, a unique identity, and speak for itself. When you have a fantastic cupcake, frosting is optional!

What about the frosting?

 Frosting and decorations can be so much fun, but they should only enhance the wonderful qualities of the cupcake that is so delicious all on its own.

Just Like Us !!!

But hold it!

Am I being compared to food?

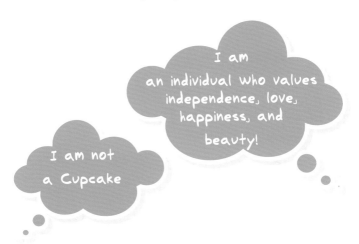

That's so very true. You are an amazing individual who encompasses all those values and so much more. But the reason you are indeed a great deal like a cupcake is

because

The best cupcakes and
the bestpeople
have Real Substance.

Let's move on from the Theory of Cupcakes to

The Cupcake

Theory...

The ♥ Cupcake Theory

 Number one

Just like a great cupcake, you too have real substance.

 Number two

You should first be your own cake, a solid foundation built from your own sense of self, happiness from within, and the ability to hold your own.

 Number three

You are the one and only you, so embrace your uniqueness and be true to yourself.

 Number four

Your partner, just like frosting, should only be an enhancement to your already solid and incredible self.

MAKING SENSE OF
The Cupcake Theory

 First there is YOU - the cake. Cake always comes first and has real substance.

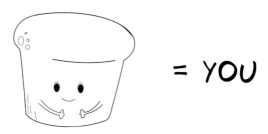 = YOU

 Then, there is YOUR PARTNER - the frosting. Frosting comes second.

 = Your partner

What does 'a cupcake should be able
to hold its own' mean?

It means finding happiness and comfort though self-reliance, yet knowing when to depend on others (every once in a while, we all need the added support of a cupcake liner).

What does 'a cupcake should have
a solid foundation' mean?

It means having your own solid values and beliefs and staying true to them without anyone or anything hindering your foundation.

What does 'a cupcake should have
a look of its own/unique identity/
speak for itself' mean?

It means being unique and proud of your appearance and identity without letting anyone blend you in with others which would eventually lead you to lose yourself.

So now ...what do these mean all together?

Cake is what sets the whole form and foundation of the cupcake. Without a firm, delicious cake, a cupcake would not be the wonderful treat we all love! The frosting is what makes the cupcake even more decadent and tasteful. When applied to humans, this means you come first, and then there is your partner. A partner should only add to the joy and delight you feel with yourself. A partner should not make you, but only add to your charm and excitement.

Making sense of
the cupcake theory

A simple guide to being happy in relationships while staying true to yourself:

The Cupcake Theory

Now for the secret recipe!

The following 10 illustrations will show various types of cupcakes with frostings and decorations. They will depict different types of relationships. These illustrations will show the importance of having balance in a relationship with a partner.

The Cupcake Theory

IN PICTURES!

Which one are you?

Can you identify yourself?
In one? In all?

In your current relationship?

Have you ever been any

of these cupcakes?

A Controlling Partner

This type of partner may first awe and impress you with decisiveness and strength, but don't let that make you forget that you are also strong and unique.

A Partner Who Loves to Have FUN

This partner can be a blast to have around, but if you're in it for the long term, make sure that he/she has goals and ambitions, too.

An Attractive Partner

This partner is indeed so wonderful to see, but don't stand in his/her shadow. Let your own unique beauty shine brightly, too!

A Discouraging Partner

Don't let this partner's gloom and doom weigh you down and hold you back. Surround yourself with positive people who will uplift and enhance you.

A Romantic Partner

This partner may give you butterflies, but be careful not to get swept away too soon. Keep your impulses in check and remember to think with your head and not just your heart.

A Needy Partner

It feels good to be needed, but this partner goes too far! Others' expectations and desires may only hold you down, but listen to your heart... you deserve to FLY!

A Vain Partner

This partner may be so absorbed in having the best and most expensive stuff to show off that there's no time and energy left for you. Make sure your partner has substance and strong inner characteristics. Don't let the extravagance fool you.

A Jealous Partner

This partner can make life miserable by limiting everything you do. Be grateful for what you have, and be even more grateful for others' great qualities that you desire to embody.

A Caring Partner

This partner is purely a gem. We all need somebody to lean on sometimes, and this partner's compassion is a comfort and treasure.

A Partner Who Loves Unconditionally

This partner celebrates your perks and accepts all your quirks!

So many kinds of frosting out there!
It might be intimidating and overwhelming
to keep in mind all of the time when it comes
to choosing your partner...

But remember,
what is most
important about
this is...

YOU!

Remember, cake
comes first.

The frosting should
only add to you,

not make you.

Are you your own cupcake?

Or are you letting the frosting
get the best of you?

Be you.

Be your own
cupcake...

Let the frosting be an enhancer
to your already solid self!

Take control of your relationship!

It's your choice.

Your Thoughts:

_____

_____

_____

_____

_____

Are you your own
cupcake?
Or are you letting
the frosting get
the best of you?

_____

_____

_____

_____

_____

Apply The Cupcake Theory in your own life and share your
own thoughts and experiences with the rest of the world on
www.cupcaketheorybook.com.

ACKNOWLEDGEMENTS

As we create our own paths and strut through this journey of life, we must remember to be grateful for those walking along beside us and strive to grow together with those who support our passions and aspirations. After all, with compassion and synergy, we can achieve the impossible and heal the world.

Coming up with this theory and actually writing this book has been a long journey full of dynamic adventures, self-realizations, collaborations, and learning. Apart from my efforts, I truly believe that the success of any project depends largely on the encouragement and guidelines of many others. I take this page to express my sincere gratitude to the fabulous people who have been instrumental in the successful completion of *The Cupcake Theory* book. I would like to show my greatest appreciation to those who provided support, read, wrote, offered comments, talked things over, allowed me to quote their endorsements and reviews, assisted in the editing, proofreading and design process. Thank you for believing in me, sharing my vision, contributing to this book, and continuing to leave a legacy in this world with your talents, passion, and wisdom.

Social Networks, *The Cupcake Theory* Book Website, Twitter, Facebook, and The Cupcake Theory Movement supporters, friends, followers, and everyone else who made this book possible: Thank you for your support and energy. We are a one global network online or offline. *The Cupcake Theory* is yours to practice and I am blessed to be here to share it with you.

Of the many fabulous cupcake connoisseurs I encountered in the last year and a half, I would like to thank the following for their full support and enthusiasm during the extensive Theory of Cupcakes research process: Kickass Cupcakes, MA: Sara Ross and Staff, LuLu's Cupcakes: Sandy Russo; Treat Cupcake, MA: Adrienne Sprague

Special Thanks to:

Forward: Robert J. Thomas, Ph.D.; Copy Editors: Linda S. Krajewski, Gina Citarella; Illustrator: Yasmeen El Dahan; Cover Design: Deasy Suryani; Endorsers and Reviewers: Janet Lever, Ph.D., Andrew Cai, Raquel Olsson, Heidi Netzley, Kenneth Elmore, Ron Buse, Cathy Vo, Barry Smith, Bonnie Weiss, Bonnie Winings, Arthur Mandel, Mike Oshins, Gabriella Valez; Photographer (cover and bio): Khiem Tran; Cupcake Contribution: Sara Ross and Staff at Kickass Cupcakes, MA

To my friends and my love,

Words cannot describe how grateful I am to have your support, memories, inspiration, and faith.

Cheers to Countless Laughter, Endless Growth, and Indescribable Love!

Thank you sincerely,

Clara.

ABOUT THE AUTHOR

 Clara Lee is the author of "*The Cupcake Theory*," a book about romantic relationships and self-worth. She was born in Seoul, Korea and raised in Northern California from age nine, before attending and graduating from Boston University where she honed her entrepreneurial spirit. Her love for the arts got her involved in the world of fashion, media and entertainment, including modeling, acting, dancing, singing and songwriting. Lee currently resides in Los Angeles with her puppy Blueberry. She divides her time between the East and West coasts in order to perform all her passions – including coaching in the fields of business, life and relationships, and maintaining her commitments to speak at various universities and events throughout the country. This is Clara's first book.

For additional information about Lee,
visit www.clarainspired.com

and

www.cupcaketheorybook.com.